PENGUIN BOOKS

VIABILITY

SARAH VAP is the author of five collections of poetry and poetics, including *Dummy Fire*, recipient of the 2006 Saturnalia Books Poetry Prize, and *American Spikenard*, recipient of the 2006 Iowa Poetry Prize. Her work has appeared in the *American Poetry Review*, *Denver Quarterly*, and *Gulf Coast*, among other publications. She lives in Venice, California.

THE NATIONAL POETRY SERIES

The National Poetry Series was established in 1978 to ensure the publication of five poetry books annually through five participating publishers. Publication is funded annually by the Lannan Foundation; Amazon Literary Partnership; Barnes & Noble; the Poetry Foundation; the PG Family Foundation; and the Betsy Community Fund; Joan Bingham, Mariana Cook, Stephen Graham, Juliet Lea Hillman Simonds, William Kistler, Jeffrey Ravetch, Laura Baudo Sillerman, and Margaret Thornton. For a complete listing of generous contributors to the National Poetry Series, please visit www.nationalpoetryseries.org.

2014 COMPETITION WINNERS

Monograph, by Simeon Berry of Somerville, MA
Chosen by Denise Duhamel for University of Georgia Press

The Regret Histories, by Joshua Poteat of Richmond, VA
Chosen by Campbell McGrath for HarperCollins

Let's Let That Are Not Yet: Inferno, by Ed Pavlić of Athens, GA
Chosen by John Keene for Fence Books

Double Jinx, by Nancy Reddy of Madison, WI
Chosen by Alex Lemon for Milkweed Editions

Viability, by Sarah Vap of Venice, CA
Chosen by Mary Jo Bang for Penguin Books

VIABILITY

SARAH VAP

PENGUIN BOOKS

PENGUIN BOOKS
An imprint of Penguin Random House LLC
375 Hudson Street
New York, New York 10014
penguin.com

LIBRARY OF CONGRESS CATALOGING-IN-PUBLICATION DATA
Vap, Sarah.
[Poems. Selections]
Viability / Sarah Vap.
pages ; cm—(National Poetry Series)
ISBN 978-0-14-312828-1
I. Title.
PS3622.A679A6 2015
813'.6—dc23
2015011853

Set in Albertina MT Std
Designed by Ginger Legato

147204767

for my father, Daniel J. Vap

1943–2014

an animal of actual mercy

The more torture went on in the basement, the more insistently they made sure the roof rested on columns.

—Adorno

Where there is no love, put love—and you will find love.

—John of the Cross

ACKNOWLEDGMENTS

These poems appeared, sometimes under a different title or in a different form, in the following publications. Grateful acknowledgment to: *The American Poetry Review, Court Green, Denver Quarterly, Gulf Coast, Marooned, Packingtown Review, Starting Today* (anthology), *Fire On Her Tongue* (anthology), *Poem-A-Day, Interim, Lingerpost, The New Census* (*Thermos* blog), *Spoon River Poetry Review.*

My gratitude:
is enormous for the many, many friends, teachers, strangers, and family who have taught and offered me their human love. Thank you to Mary Jo Bang, David St. John, Carmen Giménez Smith, Danielle Pafunda, Todd Fredson, and Norman Dubie, who helped me in very different ways with this book. Thank you to Marcia Aquino, to my parents, to Todd, Oskar, Mateo & Archie, who made writing this book possible.

VIABILITY

The splintered log filled me mouth to groin. And growing—growing, the emerald was blood. The stones in the water were eyes and I was not recognized by either the givings or the killings that will make a woman a mother, that will make a mother a moon dropped to the water and carving out her own eye. Our family was afraid for itself until we were worn. And became, at evening's porcelain quality, like even the dead dog's bones, silent and white. The infant and the carriage, frozen below the firepond—they held themselves, were alone. We looked down at them through thick ice while they ripped him from me in the single, performed loneliness.

Bloodletting: A period marked by severe investing losses. Bloodletting may occur during a bear market, in which the value of securities in many sectors may decline rapidly and heavily.

The body below my head is exploded, memory bloodlets. Remembrance, rapidly and heavily.

Hysteresis: From the Greek term meaning "a coming short, a deficiency." Hysteresis, a term coined by Sir James Alfred Ewing, a Scottish physicist and engineer (1855–1935), refers to systems, organisms and fields that have memory. In other words, the consequences of an input are experienced with a certain lag time, or delay. One example is seen with iron: iron maintains some magnetization after it has been exposed to and removed from a magnetic field. In economics, hysteresis arises when a single disturbance affects the course of the economy.

▼

Hysterical stitched together it used to be something else I don't know what. Oozing parted roughly it used to be something else I don't know what. Pulling itself toward me something needs help I don't remember what. Does it hum, it does. I listen to it hum. Does it hum, it does. I listen to it hum. Does it hum, it does: I will listen to it hum.

Hold him. An infant can't love himself, I think. Plum, magenta reversals of light—a cloth ball to roll to the infant. His is the more decent dark radiance—he is still an infant picking through a pile of yarn. He might watch the beautiful things of this world disappear. Yet where my remembrance joins his reminiscence—as scraps of paper on the floor, or a few purple tiles. Who, on the advice of her soul alone, could be the counterweight of his plain light. But the final color is different, as something permanent is. As an heir to memory is, or as a love that will hurt us.

▼

Where there is no love, put love—and you will find love. Where there is no memory, put memory—and you will find memory. Where there is no pull, put iron filings, put metal, put bindings, put jaw-traps wide open, and there you will find the pull.

—John of the Cross

Leading Lipstick Indicator: An indicator based on the theory that a consumer turns to less expensive indulgences, such as lipstick, when she feels less than confident about the future. Therefore, lipstick sales tend to increase during times of economic uncertainty or a recession. Also known as the "lipstick effect."

This term was coined by Leonard Lauder (chairman of Estée Lauder), who consistently found that during tough economic times, his lipstick sales went up. Believe it or not, the indicator has been quite a reliable signal of consumer attitudes over the years. For example, in the months following the September 11 terrorist attacks, lipstick sales doubled.

▼

Breathing loaf of wild animal, give, I said to you once. Paint my eyes black at their edges. Blue powder that glows in the grease. Did I say it when I held our son up above my head laughing so hard my milk fell out of his mouth to the edge of my eye. But who would hear of blackened milk or of this joy, we are tired of women and children. Tired of a woman's painted eye which has not stopped us, and God has not stopped us. The possibility is different where free and wild have lived in the adoring mind. The blackening woods at evening are beside me, pulling rabbits. Pulling rabbits.

What do we mean by "efficiency"? Essentially, we shall mean a comparison of the return from the use of this form of capital—Negro slaves—with the returns being earned on other capital assets at the time. Thus we mean to consider whether the slave system was being dragged down of its own weight; whether the allocation of resources was impaired by the rigidity of capitalized labor supply; whether southern capital was misused or indeed drawn away to the North; and, finally, whether slavery must inevitably have declined from an inability of the slave force to reproduce itself.

▼

Where there is inability, put worth dragging down one's own weight. Where capital is misused and drawn away, put more inability. Slavery's failure is the fault of slavery's inability—put much more fault, put membranes between the faults, and there you will find your inability.

—John of the Cross

To survive this, she whispers, *this world*. Her love lasts into the slipped marriage of her precisions—Latin, *precis*, is prayer. *Precarios*: the precious thing. Does the precious thing hum, it does. Does the precarious thing hum, it does.

In what ways was slavery allegedly responsible for the drain of capital from the South? The major avenues by which wealth is said to have been drained from the cotton states were the excessive use of credit and the "absorption" of capital in slaves.

I was looking for ways to help my family. This broker knew I was looking for work. He said he could find me a job in Thailand. All I had to do was pay a 12,000 baht fee. There was probably around 700 of us. Old men, teenage girls, everyone. We travelled in a convoy in pick-up trucks. Then we trekked for days through the jungle. There was no food. Some died on the way, others got left behind. When I saw the fishing boats, I realised I'd been sold.

▼

Where there is no doubling, put rabbits—put lipstick. There you will find increase. Where lipstick, put absorption. Where absorption, put women. There is no reason to make this more difficult than it is. In what way is slavery responsible for the drain of capital from the South? Is this the question? Want increase, put increase, find increase.

—John of the Cross

Bo Derek: A slang term used to describe a perfect stock or investment. In the 1979 hit movie *10*, actress Bo Derek portrayed the "perfect woman," or "the perfect 10." This term was used more often in the early 1980s, after the movie *10* first came out. Nowadays, the name of a more current celebrity, like Jennifer Lopez, might be used in finance jargon.

Was the southerner his own victim in an endless speculative inflation of slave prices?

It seems that the parlous state of fish stocks and the pressure to monitor supply chains for sustainability has made the issue of slavery visible. Two retailers who did not wish to be named said that when they started to look at where fish for prawn feed was coming from, it became clear that the boats engaged in illegal fishing were also likely to be using trafficked forced labour.

Where there is no love, put information. There you will find the algorithm. Put even more information. The algorithm will increase. Everything you want will increase.

—John of the Cross

Where there is no speculation, put inflation—and you will find love's victim. Put the victim. Put operations all across the victim. Put very quiet calls for each other. If I understand, what we want here is an increase.

—John of the Cross

▼

Night, two months along. I wanted an infant, I put an infant, and so there I will find an infant. I imagine we are together right now. Your fingers, we will sleep. Our daydreams— wishing for you across all of time's thickness—across all of dark water and into entire night. Toothless and devout, the wormhole you could slip through. No light at all untelling our quietest calls for each other within the small time that we could be given. Darkness. Quiet. A speed, excessively given. Infant, our worlds are almost held together, will help be given.

The Halo Effect: A term used in marketing to explain the bias shown by customers towards certain products because of a favorable experience with other products made by the same manufacturer or maker. Basically, the halo effect is driven by brand equity.

The opposite of the halo effect is "cannibalization."

Where there is no cannibalization, put wire—and you will find wire. Where there is no cannibalization, put memory—and you will find mind. Where there is no wire halo, put wire wrapped tightly around a mind. Put wire wrapped tightly around a torso. Put wire wrapped tightly around many bodies at the same time. Where there are no saints, put cannibalization—put body upon body—and there you will find even more.

—John of the Cross

Daydream: The infant becomes several large fish inside me, my mouth tastes like fishwater. I ooze fish, feel the fish churn and surge from vagina to tonsils they are becoming desperate. They want to escape out my throat I gag and I want, I whisper to you, to puke large, whole fishes. I want fishes up my throat and out my mouth. I want all my teeth to scrape at the scales as the fish swim up my throat and out my mouth. I want a paste of scales and blood to gather along the backs of all my teeth as the fish move up my throat and out my mouth. I am convulsing with maniac fish when the heat of my body turns on: the fish are stilling. The fish are boiling. The fish are dying I am the one doing it.

To the extent that profitability is a necessary condition for the continuation of a private business institution in a free-enterprise society, slavery was not untenable in the ante bellum American South.

Extensive overfishing in the Gulf of Thailand has forced Thai fleets to travel further afield for longer periods to meet market demands. According to UN estimates, roughly 40% of all Thailand's seafood is now being caught in foreign waters, from Malaysia and Indonesia all the way out towards Papua New Guinea to the east and Bangladesh to the west.

Coupled with mounting petrol prices, this overfishing has led to ever-decreasing profit margins for Thai boat captains, says Human Rights Watch's Robertson: "What motivates is not concern for fishermen's welfare, but rather maximising catch and ensuring profitability, and that means 18- to 22-hour work days and martial discipline to keep men working."

Untenable? Where there is no love, put continuation or put increase or put proliferation—and there you will find the love untenable. Language is not infinity. Language is not hopeful. There is no rapture in language. Language is always doing. Language is never undoing. I admit that I had hoped to "love" and "be loved."

—John of the Cross

Skirt Length Theory: The idea that skirt lengths are a predictor of the stock market direction. According to the theory, if skirts are short, it means the markets are going up. And if skirts are long, it means the markets are heading down. Also called the Hemline Theory.

The idea behind this theory is that shorter skirts tend to appear in times when general consumer confidence and excitement is high, meaning the markets are bullish. In contrast, the theory says long skirts are worn more in times of fear and general gloom, indicating that things are bearish.

Although some investors may secretly believe in such a theory, serious analysts and investors—instead of examining skirt length to make investment decisions—insist on focusing on market fundamentals and data.

▼

The actual bear is in a skirt. The actual bull is a saint. The actual fish is a multibillion-dollar industry. The actual skirt is a fundamental. What do you secretly believe in? What do you secretly want? Me—if I could conceive, I could increase.

—John of the Cross

Where there is no information, put information—put operations—the algorithm is unbreakable. The algorithm is thinking.

—John of the Cross

I examine the infant for breathing does it hum, it does. I examine my father for breathing does he hum, he does. There is a hum, therefore, at each end of my memory, and where there is memory there is the love cannibalizing the memory. My father is dying my infant might live. They are both in the same doorway. They are in the same light.

Cash Cow: 1. One of the four categories (quadrants) in the BCG growth-share matrix that represents the division within a company that has a large market share within a mature industry.

2. A business, product or asset that, once acquired and paid off, will produce consistent cash flow over its lifespan. A cash cow requires little investment capital and perennially provides positive cash flows, which can be allocated to other divisions within the corporation. These cash generators may also use their money to buy back shares on the market or pay dividends to shareholders.

Cash cow is a metaphor for a dairy cow that produces milk over the course of its life and requires little maintenance. A dairy cow is an example of a cash cow, as after the initial capital outlay has been paid off, the animal continues to produce milk for many years to come.

This swell and then my throat's warm collapse—and love's holler collapsed . . . mouthful, full of the warming, oh, valentine. Long, and left better collapsed along the lover. Warm, and left better, collapsed along my caw. The caws, thermonuclear, left open left seeping around us.

Of the 15 current and former slaves the *Guardian* interviewed during the investigation, 10 had witnessed a fellow fisherman murdered by his boat captain or net master. Ei Ei Lwin, the Burmese fisherman, claims he saw "18 to 20 people killed in front of me."

But where are the animals of actual praise. Where are the animals of actual mercy. Where is the coin in the animal. Where is the coin in the infant and where is the infant in the infant animal.

—John of the Cross

I want fusion, as in a joining together. As in confusion. As in thermonuclear. I want to become mixed together with something infinite, together at my smallest and my greatest part. Fused, for example, with exponential growth. Fused with exponential decay—or fused with the passage of fish across time. Fused with the generous field, leaning always toward me. Or fused with the animals of increase.

—John of the Cross

From the standpoint of the entrepreneur making an investment in slaves, the basic problems involved in determining profitability are analytically the same as those met in determining the returns from any other kind of capital investment. The acquisition of a slave represented the tying-up of capital in what has appropriately been called a roundabout method of production. Like the purchase of any capital, a slave purchase was made in the anticipation of gaining higher returns than are available from less time-consuming or capital-using methods. This model is particularly applicable in the present case, because slave investments, like the forests or wine cellars of classic capital theory, produced a natural increase with the passage of time.

Daydream: Wire is wrapped around my torso—line exactly under line exactly under line from my collarbone to my hips. No skin shows the wire is so exactly wrapped and I can just barely expand my lungs to breathe. With the natural passage of time the infant will grow. This is a kind of natural increase. As the infant grows it will be crushed. The wire will not give and I will not give.

Stillborn god, will you rip your own body to hold your share of what hurts—as Columbus ran the Santa Maria aground a reef of Hispaniola. On Christmas Day she foundered, and Columbus built La Navidad, a military fortress, from her remains. So even in human terms we are no longer what we were. The comfort we need is inhuman. The curtain of water, incessant. The curtain of water, incessant.

Goodwill: An intangible asset that arises as a result of the acquisition of one company by another for a premium value. The value of a company's brand name, solid customer base, good customer relations, good employee relations and any patents or proprietary technology represent goodwill. Goodwill is considered an intangible asset because it is not a physical asset like buildings or equipment. The goodwill account can be found in the assets portion of a company's balance sheet.

Where there is no goodwill, put acquisition. Put incessant proprietary technology. Where there is no goodwill, put cannibalization. Put host. Put incarnation. Put transmutation. Where there is no love, put abstract animals. Where there is no love, put lipstick. Put mascara. Put lipstick down the throat of the rat. Put hairspray up the nose of the rat. Put hairspray into the lungs of the rat. Where there is no love, put lipstick on abstract animals.

—John of the Cross

Either the infant is assimilated or else he is annihilated. Either the infant is extracted or else he is disgorged. Asleep on top of me his mouth is soggy and open, so open my heart hurts. A fetal curl pressed into me, face in my armpit because if he can't smell me he can't sleep. He roots, grunts, until my nipple is in his mouth. Still asleep, he rubs my other breast while he sucks. He is not hidden from me because I won't understand but hidden from me absolutely.

Jennifer Lopez: A slang technical analysis term referring to a rounding bottom in a stock's price pattern. This term got its name from Jennifer Lopez's curvy figure; she is often criticized (or praised) for her round bottom.

Traders like the rounding bottom in a stock pattern because it can be an indication of a positive market reversal, meaning expectations are gradually shifting from bearish to bullish.

Some were shot, others were tied up to stones and thrown into the sea, and one was ripped apart, he says. A fisherman hated his captain and tried to beat him to death. But the captain escaped by jumping into the sea. The other captains came and pinned the fisherman down. Then they tied up his hands and legs to four separate boats and pulled him apart.

There is a pink light through Tamar's veil. There is a stone quality to time—when the poorest cannot make their bodies good. A woman's body is a list of hard facts. How it feels and what it has done shivering with seed, I am his mother. Also lifted, also laughing, also smeared across the substances.

A bear's body is a list of hard facts about her body. A bull's body is a list of hard facts about her body. A man's body is a list of hard facts about her body. A man's body should outperform its competition.

—John of the Cross

Angelina Jolie Stock Index: An index made up of a selection of stocks from companies associated with actress Angelina Jolie. Seen as one of the world's most influential celebrities, some analysts believe that companies connected with Jolie will outperform their competition.

The index was created by Fred Fuld of Stockerblog.com; it includes the stocks of movie studios and producers that have had a connection with Angelina Jolie, such as Sony (NYSE: SNE), Viacom (NYSE: VIA) and Time Warner (NYSE: TWX). Because Jolie's films usually earn large box-office revenues, the companies that produce these movies should have higher profits.

Index, put actual bears, put actual bulls, put actual cows, put actual lipstick on the actual animals of real earth.

—John of the Cross

▼

Index, put the shivering seed in earth, put the climbing vine around the torso of the golden goose, put Jack in the pot of the giant or put Hansel in the pot of the witch or put infants in the pot of actual earth.

—John of the Cross

Index, I don't have the authority.

—John of the Cross

The inefficiency argument is not supported very securely. There were slaves employed in cotton factories throughout the South. Slaves were used in the coal mines and in the North Carolina lumbering operations. In the ironworks at Richmond and on the Cumberland River, slaves comprised a majority of the labor force. Southern railroads were largely built by southern slaves. Crop diversification, or the failure to achieve diversification, appears to have been a problem of entrepreneurship rather than of the difficulties of training slaves. In the face of the demand for cotton and the profits to be had from specializing in this single crop, it is hardly difficult to explain the single-minded concentration of the planter.

Index, in the face of the difficulty of training slaves, put crop diversification. In the face of the difficulty of training slaves, put demand for cotton, put single-minded concentration. Put a body between four boats. Put your hands in the gesture of prayer. Put your body in the gesture of cowering. Put your face in the expression of an animal.

—John of the Cross

In the glow of the planet earth night-light the infant has dissolved earth's favor: he is a speck among the specks we've missed. The crystal fringe of the wedding dress is a simple column of glass blown from the volcano—infant. He who could emerge whole into the world. Earth, the sky is your white knight—his hands are cupped toward you in the ancient gesture of need.

Globalization: The tendency of investment funds and businesses to move beyond domestic and national markets to other markets around the globe, thereby increasing the interconnectedness of different markets. Globalization has had the effect of markedly increasing not only international trade, but also cultural exchange.

The advantages and disadvantages of globalization have been heavily scrutinized and debated in recent years. Proponents of globalization say that it helps developing nations "catch up" to industrialized nations much faster through increased employment and technological advances. Critics of globalization say that it weakens national sovereignty and allows rich nations to ship domestic jobs overseas where labor is much cheaper.

Daydream: I am lying naked on my back on the floor. Strangers walk through the room, one after another, and step on my belly. They are wearing white clothes and no shoes and some balance, bounce, then step off. Some stomp. My belly is huge. Exposed. I am a giant and made up almost only of my own eyes. As they pass over us, another, another, I can feel the infant's legs arms head push out into my lungs and into my throat and against the cage of my bones stressed almost to cracking, another. Another in the light of the doorway. The line of people extends as far as I can see. At each step we are more deformed. The room is dark the strangers are endless and I don't seem to stop them.

▼

"Ghost boats"—unlicensed replicas of properly registered and licensed boats—make up as much as half of Thailand's true fishing fleet, according to a 2011 International Organisation for Migration report.

"There's a technique," a high-ranking marine police officer in Kantang, on the Andaman coast, told the *Guardian*. "If you have 10 boats, you buy a licence for just two or three boats. Then you'll have two boats with the same name, and two with no name." He chuckles. "If they get stopped, they have a licence to show the authorities, but really it's a fake licence."

Lady Godiva Accounting Principles (LGAP): A theoretical set of accounting principles under which corporations would have to fully disclose all information, including that which often doesn't get reported to investors under generally accepted accounting principles (GAAP).

These principles include disclosure of the following:

- all off–balance sheet items
- how new goodwill accounting rules (introduced in 2002) impact earnings per share (EPS)
- the impact on EPS of stock options issued in lieu of salaries
- how pension expenses are accounted for

This buzzword was coined by financial analyst Rick Wayman after the Enron bankruptcy.

According to legend, Lady Godiva was a woman who rode a horse naked through Coventry, England, in the 11th century in order to get her husband, the Lord of Coventry, to lift the heavy taxes on his people. The idea of LGAP is that just as the Lady provided "full disclosure" to help her fellow citizens, corporations must do the same thing with their financial disclosures to maintain their credibility with investors.

Daydream: Amidst all this lovemaking God and animals must enter, if she then crosses her thighs it becomes a "circle." If, in the "mare's trap," which can only be done with practice, she grasps him like a mare so tightly that he cannot move.

Where there is no God, put full-disclosures. Where there is no circle, put full-disclosures, full-disclosures so tightly that you cannot move.

—John of the Cross

Slave longevity corresponds, of course, to the period for which a slave investment was made. Looking back at the data in Table 1, there is no reason to expect twenty-year-old Massachusetts Negroes to have a lower life-expectancy than Massachusetts whites, though both clearly lived longer than southern Negroes of the period. Taking all these factors into account, an estimate of thirty to thirty-five years of life-expectancy seems most plausible for twenty-year-old Negroes working as prime cotton hands on southern plantations in the period 1830–50, and a thirty-year life-expectancy will generally be used in the succeeding calculations.

Gush, the long pink ribbon. The long skin-pudding shaken out—my sympathy comes from my body. The baby's old brain and new brain, without the sense burnt or built, are terrible into the light—or thoroughly we believe otherwise. The catastrophe of my body for the body I surround—the fish-human with a fever mark on its cheek. These are the years, "childbearing," when things will live or die and inside of us. How still is this reciprocity: to let alone something that I might have touched.

This is capitalism at its worst, and it is supported by a dramatic alteration in the basic economic equation of slavery. Where an average slave in 1850 would have cost the equivalent of $40,000 in modern money, today's slave can be bought for a few hundred dollars. This cheapness makes the modern slave easily affordable, but it also makes him or her a disposable commodity.

Gadfly: A slang term for an investor who attends the annual shareholders meeting to criticize the corporation's executives. A gadfly addresses many issues for the shareholders, often grilling the management by asking difficult or embarrassing questions.

Named after small insects that bite and annoy livestock, the gadfly looks to irritate a corporation's management until it acts on shareholder concerns. Questions regarding executive compensation or inconvenient annual meeting locations are often brought to light by a gadfly. A gadfly adds value for other shareholders by vocalizing their concerns and inciting action.

With one glass I've trapped a roach over the drain. While it thinks, I crawl on the floor searching for the rattle and bits of the other glass that I broke—their secret alignments, I know you have heard this: a secret. It feels like a secret I'll carve out more deeply with this infant. To talk to you of the infant is to talk to you about God with the awe spinning or dropping from the mother of this house. You won't forget me, when I lift this glass, and I won't forget you.

It is also frequently argued that slavery gave southern planters a taste for extravagant, wasteful display, causing the notorious lack of thrift and the relative lack of economic development, compared to that experienced in the North and West. This is a doubtful inference, at best. Slavery did not make the Cavalier any more than slavery invented speculation in cotton.

Slavery did not make the Cavalier! Slavery does not make extravagance! Slavery does not reproduce itself quickly enough. Slavery does not make the Southern planter do anything he doesn't already want to do—does slavery have that kind of Index?

—John of the Cross

Is the Index actually a woman who could love us? Is the Index actually an infant to sell? Think about it that way.

—John of the Cross

How does the Index love us? The Index loves us like we are its infant and its meal. The Index loves us like we are its labor and its fuck. The Index loves us like we are its information and its surface upon which to reflect an image of the Index. The Index loves us like we are its lipstick and its mother. The Index loves us like we are slaves with the ability to reproduce ourselves.

—John of the Cross

Eva Longoria Stock Index: A stock index comprised of companies related to the actress Eva Longoria. Some analysts believe that Eva Longoria has enough influence over consumers that her endorsements will materially affect product sales.

On the popular television show *Desperate Housewives* Longoria often promotes consumer goods. Outside of acting, she has endorsement deals with companies such as Hanes (NYSE: HBI), Bebe (NASDAQ: BEBE) and L'Oréal (NASDAQ: LRLCY). These companies are included in the Eva Longoria Stock Index, under the premise that her fans will increase the revenues of the promoted products.

Put all of your money in the Eva Longoria Stock Index. Put all of your money in the Angelina Jolie Stock Index. Put all of your money in the Lindsay Lohan Stock Index. Put all of your money in the Jennifer Lopez Stock Index. Put all of your money in the Paris Hilton Stock Index. Put it into the tender membranes of their Index, put it into their pink and lavender membranes, put it into their weapons-grade membranes that are holding our worlds together.

—John of the Cross

A single membrane separated me from the infant whose horizon was simple: a sheet of light. The surface that held our worlds together. Strong fat legs—he stands. But the other who left in the blood, left while you wrapped the leftover cake in the old cloth diaper that we use for a rag.

After being warned for four consecutive years that it was not doing enough to tackle slavery within its borders, Thailand now risks being downgraded to the lowest ranking on the US State Department's human trafficking index, which evaluates 188 nations according to how well they combat and prevent human trafficking. A relegation to Tier 3 would put Thailand on a par with North Korea and Iran, and could lead to a downgrade in Thailand's trading status with the US.

According to the Global Slavery Index, nearly 500,000 people are believed to be currently enslaved within Thailand's borders—and a significant number of them are likely to be out at sea.

We said that love is an almost-unimaginable proliferation, is the daughter-product of love. Love, we said, yields. Love is the generous field that bends toward me, the radiance during the blast. We said that love increases as memory increases. We measured love in tiers and tables and in equivalent megatons. We measured love, and love increased.

Absolute Advantage: The ability of a country, individual, company or region to produce a good or service at a lower cost per unit than the cost at which any other entity produces that good or service. Entities with absolute advantages can produce a product or service using a smaller number of inputs and/or using a more efficient process than another party producing the same product or service. Here is an example of how absolute advantage works:

Jane can knit a sweater in 10 hours, while Kate can knit a sweater in 8 hours. Kate has an absolute advantage over Jane, because it takes her fewer hours (the input) to produce a sweater (the output).

An entity can have an absolute advantage in more than one good or service. Absolute advantage also explains why it makes sense for countries, individuals and businesses to trade with one another. Because each has advantages in producing certain products and services, they can both benefit from trade. For example:

Jane can produce a painting in 5 hours while Kate needs 9 hours to produce a comparable painting. Jane has an absolute advantage over Kate in painting. Remember Kate has an absolute advantage over Jane in knitting sweaters. If both Jane and Kate specialize in the products they have an absolute advantage in and buy the products they don't have an absolute advantage in from the other entity, they will both be better off.

Less, and less, to love. Of ourselves, too. We have tried everything. Children waiting in a horoscope, the tips of a ministerial light—*Temperance* crossed by the knight in our Tarot. Very soon, his teeth will emerge one by one. You will pound them in a circle to the side of the barn, and wait for the sun to strike it. To mark it with another B.

Where there is no love, put love—and you will find love. Put wire.

—John of the Cross

▼

Where there is no love, put wire—and you will refine love.

—John of the Cross

Falling Knife: A slang phrase for a security or industry in which the current price or value has dropped significantly in a short period of time.

This term implies that the investment will never be a good one again.

Daydream: I am grotesquely huge so that when I lean over to pick up my teacup the pressure makes the blood of my body fall out my mouth. Fall smoothly, like buckets of blood simply falling. My body deflates as the pressure of all the blood falling increases: now blood from my mouth like blood from a fire hose—blood sprays and my face is thrown back from the force. Now I'm heaving blood. I'm heaving and my mouth, open wide, is *pouring*—pausing—*pouring*. The teacup in my hand as blood is falling. Blood down the walls and over the floor as blood is falling. I'm soaked with blood and the room is soaking up blood when human teeth fill the blood.

The price of slaves fluctuated widely, being subject to the waves of speculation in cotton. Furthermore, the price depended, among other things, upon the age, sex, disposition, degree of training, and condition of the slave. In order to hold these variables roughly constant, we shall confine our present analysis to eighteen–twenty-year-old prime field hands and wenches. Some summary data on slave prices were compiled by U. B. Phillips on the basis of available market quotations, bills of transactions, and reports of sales in most of the important slave markets of Georgia. His estimates of the best averages for several years between 1828 and 1860 are presented in Table 2. On the basis of these data it would appear that both the median and the mean price for prime field hands were in the range of from $900 to $950 in the period 1830–50.

Where there is no love, put infants in Table 2. Put angels in Table 1. Where there is no love, put the best averages. Where there is no love, put infants in most of the important slave markets. Where there is no love, where there are no angels, put infants or put no infants—and there you will still find no love. There is some increase in infant radiance.

—John of the Cross

Angel investors are high-net-worth individuals who deploy their own funds to provide startup capital to promising early-stage ventures. Silicon Valley, where many of the world's biggest technology companies got their start, is home to numerous archangels.

One infant had his start when he was carved quietly out, and the other, his little trucks covering the table while we wait. Is it better to say lost than to write it—the burn until he cooled inside of a hospital, inside cure's humiliations.

Life on a 15-metre trawler is brutal, violent and unpredictable. Many of the slaves interviewed by the *Guardian* recalled being fed just a plate of rice a day. Men would take fitful naps in sleeping quarters so cramped they would crawl to enter them, before being summoned back out to trawl fish at any hour. Those who were too ill to work were thrown overboard, some interviewees reported, while others said they were beaten if they so much as took a lavatory break.

Put acute exposure. Put luminosity at a maximum. Put official registration, put a conglomerate, put annual revenue of more than $30 billion, put 500,000 tons of shrimp a year, put an Ocean Health Index.

—John of the Cross

▼

Where there is no infant, put Americium—there you will find the infant radiating.

—John of the Cross

Americium (pronounced AM-ə-RISH-ee-əm) is a radioactive transuranic chemical element with symbol Am and atomic number 95. This member of the actinide series is located in the periodic table under the lanthanide element europium, and thus by analogy was named after another continent, America.

The longest-lived and most common isotopes of americium, ^{241}Am and ^{243}Am, have half-lives of 432.2 and 7,370 years, respectively. Therefore, any primordial americium (americium that was present on Earth during its formation) should have decayed by now.

Existing americium is concentrated in the areas used for the atmospheric nuclear weapons tests conducted between 1945 and 1980, as well as at the sites of nuclear incidents, such as the Chernobyl disaster.

Where there is no love, put infant—there you will find the money radiating.

—John of the Cross

▼

Love Money: Seed money or capital given by family or friends to an entrepreneur to start a business. The decision to lend money and the terms of the agreement are usually based on qualitative factors and the relationship between the two parties, rather than on a formulaic risk analysis.

Storm. You pronounce it out loud, like to a dog—*stop*. Turn. Unstoppably, the living one sleeps. His rest was as bare as my memory of that snow, or as a warning—and the whole tree sparkles across the road. We are trying to return home from the hospital when irrigation pipes also curl over the roads like we imagine the DNA curls. The road is pure gold glass at sunset. He is silent behind us, the monsters of his sleep are gone, the sky is buried, finally, everything gone.

▼

Seasons: The current stage of a proposed business idea or concept. Seasons is a slang term that is generally used among venture capitalists. The seasons are spring (infancy), summer (adolescence), fall (maturing) and winter (mature).

But, despite the fact that the problem is ostensibly one in economic history, no attempt has ever been made to measure the profitability of slavery according to the economic (as opposed to accounting) concept of profitability. This paper is an attempt to fill this void.

Where there is a void, there you will find the Index. There you will find relentlessness. There you will find proliferation. But was that a void to be filled? That was not a void to be filled? Did you think that was a void to be filled? Is that what the Index told you?

—John of the Cross

Sentiment Indicator: A graphical or numerical indicator designed to show how a group feels about the market, business environment or other factor. A sentiment indicator seeks to quantify how various factors, such as unemployment, inflation, macroeconomic conditions or politics, influence future behavior.

▼

Root, relentless. Little dream, you offer your ghost of an answer . . . are you pitiless? I have called you. Come. We'll all—that I cannot, right now, remember we will.

Billionaire: An individual who has assets or a net worth of at least one billion currency units such as dollars, euros or pounds. Each year, *Forbes* magazine publishes a list of the world's billionaires. When *Forbes* produced the first list in 1987, there were 140 names on the list. Twenty-five years later, in 2012, the list had grown to 1,226, an all-time high. Twenty-four of the billionaires on the original 1987 list remained on the list for 2012.

According to the 2012 *Forbes* report, there are billionaires from 58 countries, with the most coming from the United States, Russia and mainland China. As of 2012, some of the world's wealthiest billionaires included Carlos Slim Helú (net worth: $69 billion, source: telecommunications), Bill Gates ($61 billion, Microsoft), Warren Buffett ($44 billion, Berkshire Hathaway) and Bernard Arnault ($41 billion, LVMH).

Monster coined, and the persistent thought at the back of the mind, at the front of the mind: what about the money. What about the health. What about the money. What about the health. What about the actual care for the actual infant. What about the actual health. What about the actual money to buy the animal to feed the infant.

The infant will, in time, rub clean—like an old gold coin smoothed of its ruler. Of an almost mythical completeness. A simple cut. A severing will follow the slope that returns him to the shame of all real love. Operation, if this were meant to happen gently. Operation, if the infant has a shelf-life. If the infant has a half-life. If the infant becomes a trained muscle. If a billionaire became this infant's fragility, radiating.

Anti-Fragility: A postulated antithesis to fragility where high-impact events or shocks can be beneficial. Anti-fragility is a concept developed by professor, former trader and former hedge fund manager Nassim Nicholas Taleb. Taleb coined the term "anti-fragility" because he thought the existing words used to describe the opposite of "fragility," such as "robustness," were inaccurate. Anti-fragility goes beyond robustness; it means that something does not merely withstand a shock but actually improves because of it.

For example, he describes an anti-fragile trading strategy as one that does not merely withstand a turbulent market but becomes more appealing under such conditions. Another example he gives is weight lifting, which trains muscles not just to withstand heavy lifting but to develop increased strength as the body repairs the muscle fiber tears.

▼

At various points along the way, checkpoints are passed and officials bribed—with Thai border police often playing an integral role.

"Police and brokers—the way I see it—we're business partners," explains the broker, who claims to have trafficked thousands of migrants into Thailand over the past five years. "We have officers working on both sides of the Thai-Burmese border. If I can afford the bribe, I let the cop sit in the car and we take the main road."

Lindsay Lohan Stock Index: A stock index comprised of companies associated with actress Lindsay Lohan. Investors might correlate the popularity of Lohan with increased sales surrounding her related products. Firms involved with Lohan endorsements, advertising or movies are included in the index.

Fans may see Lindsay Lohan use a certain product, such as her Mercedes-Benz, and rush to purchase one for themselves. The increased demand will usually drive up a company's sales, merely for being associated with Lohan. Companies involved in the index include Disney (NYSE: DIS), who produce many of Lohan's films, Daimler Chrysler (NYSE: DCX) and Mattel (NASDAQ: MAT).

As with most celebrity-related terms, buzzwords such as this usually have a shorter shelf life and may become irrelevant.

Where there is no love. Where there is no love. Where there are no super-angels. Where there is no blast wave. Where there is no cooling pool. Where there is no half-life. Where there are no trash-fish. Where there is no by-catch. Where there is no inedible or infant species of fish. Where there is no fragility. Where there is no curve. Where there is no Index. Where there are no women. Where there is no animal. Where there is no price. Where there is no infant. Where there is no infant. Where there is no infant. Where there is no infant in the cooling pond. Where there is no infant.

—John of the Cross

The evidence employed in this debate has been provided by the few, usually fragmentary, accounting records that have come down to us from early plantation activities. The opposing parties have arranged and rearranged the data in accordance with various standard and sometimes imaginary accounting conventions. Indeed, the debate over the value of the different constituent pieces of information reconstructs in embryo much of the historical development of American accounting practices.

Where there is no embryo, put bikinis. Where there is no embryo, reconstruct the Embryo of American Accounting Practices. Put actual animals into the embryo. Put bears. Put cows. Put chickens. Put all the inedible and infant fish into the embryo. Put shrimp into the embryo. Put animals into bikinis. Put them into the embryo. Put americium into the embryo. Put High-Level Waste into the embryo. Put uranium-235 into the embryo. Put plutonium-239 into the embryo. Put tritium into the embryo. Put Bikini Atoll into the embryo. Radiate the embryo, and there you will find the Embryo of American Accounting Practices.

—John of the Cross

▼

Night, the three of us watch, holding hands, a children's roller coaster in the shape of a dragon, and you say: As if someone could disappear without residue. Without a stain of love somewhere on earth. Christ salted his fish. He tore the column of bones out along its back—perhaps I once believed you were knowable. You tell our son the story of the talking babydoll, cooked into a loaf of bread that hollers *Mama, Mama* from the oven. The babydoll the dragon and Jesus, you say, are each the other's world entire. It's better, simply, to say that now we know each other. To say that now I can whisper something to you, and it didn't hurt.

Speaking on condition of anonymity, a high-ranking broker explained to the *Guardian* how Thai boat owners phone him directly with their "order": the quantity of men they need and the amount they're willing to pay for them.

▼

Animal Spirits: A term used by John Maynard Keynes in one of his economics books. In his 1936 publication, *The General Theory of Employment, Interest, and Money,* the term "animal spirits" is used to describe human emotion that drives consumer confidence. According to Keynes, animal spirits also generate human trust.

There has been a resurgence of interest in the idea of animal spirits in recent years. Several books and articles have been published on this topic. Keynes believed that animal spirits were necessary to motivate people to take positive action.

From this statement of the problem, it is obvious that the following information is needed to determine the profitability of slaveholding from the slaveholder's point of view: (*a*) the longevity of slaves; (*b*) the costs of slaves and any necessary accompanying capital investments; (*c*) the interest rate; and (*d*) the annual returns from slave productive activities, defined to include both field labor and procreation.

If we need to determine the profitability of slaveholding from the slaveholder's point of view, if we need use the word procreation, if animal spirits motivate people to take positive action, if animal spirits also generate human trust, if the wire that the Index has wrapped around the animal spirits were also the rigging of the Santa Maria, if the wood from the Santa Maria was used to build the fortress called La Navidad, if La Navidad refers to the birth of the infant who grew to the man we are to eat eternally or is it relentlessly, if the wire wrapped around the animal spirits is wrapped also around the animals, wrapped also around the infants, wrapped also around the continents, wrapped also around the most important slave markets, wrapped also around the brains, wrapped also around the mouth, shoved also into the vagina, wrapped also around the testicles, hanging also from the anuses, tied also to each of the four boats, is eternal or is it relentless.

—John of the Cross

Daydream: Whimpering is a nasal sound, rising above the throat and nose, sweetly echoing. Groaning is like the deep rumble of a cloud, coming out of the throat. Crying is well known, and should be heartrending. Panting is another name for "sighing." Explain babbling, shrieking, and sobbing. These seven are indistinct sounds. Modes of slapping and the accompanying moaning. There are eight kinds of screaming: whimpering, groaning, babbling, crying, panting, shrieking, or sobbing. At this I babble. With sounds inside my mouth, and then I sob.

Our fuck descends in a heap. You say: leave it in the story. You say: don't talk about the infant that way. We say what is relentless versus what is eternal. We say: what is eternal versus what is relentless.

Weak Sister: An element that undermines the entire system. Weak sister can refer to either a single individual or a specialized group considered to be the weak link in an integrated process.

Usually referring to an undependable member of a group environment, the weak sister can also be a malfunctioning part of a team-oriented task. For example, the slowest member in an assembly line or a slow marketing team which hinders the overall performance of operations is referred to as the weak sister.

▼

The flock descends in a heap. As a major part of moaning she may use, according to her imagination, the cries of the dove, cuckoo, green pigeon, parrot, bee, nightingale, goose, duck, and partridge—which can be accessed on demand.

War Chest: A colloquial term for the reserves of cash set aside or built up by a company to take advantage of an unexpected opportunity. While a war chest is typically used for acquisitions of other companies or businesses, it can also be used as a buffer against adverse events during uncertain times. A war chest is often invested in liquid short-term investments, such as treasury bills and bank deposits, which can be accessed on demand.

Index, lift me, raise me up. Index, I want to know you. Index, increase and increase me. Open the lid during this uncertain time. Radiate inside me.

—John of the Cross

War Risk: 1. The possibility that an investment will lose value because of a major, violent political upheaval. War generates uncertainty in the financial markets and causes many investors to panic and sell, which leads to a decline in prices.

2. The possibility that an individual or company will experience a major financial loss related to the destruction of property caused by a major, violent political upheaval.

Standard insurance policies do not always cover acts of war; in some cases, it may be necessary to purchase separate war risk insurance.

▼

Smear a small red spider, a cleaning fire. If the world begins with a word, it will end with someone reciting her memory— *love lasts.* The infant's breath moves with my father's breathing machine. His fat hand is curled tightly around the cord. My father turns his head, laughs in his sleep, gently to my son's ear.

Suicide Pill: A defensive strategy by which a target company engages in an activity that might actually ruin the company rather than prevent the hostile takeover. Suicide pills are extreme actions that differ from situation to situation, some of which result in dissolving the company; however, the underlying intent is to avoid the hostile takeover of the firm by any means necessary.

Also known as the "Jonestown Defense."

▼

And to the extent that the old planting aristocracy used the profits to maintain the real or fancied magnificence of the preceding century, capital was absorbed. Slavery made this possible, so long as the natural increase could be shipped off.

They mean infants. When they say "natural increase" they mean infants. They mean proliferation.

—John of the Cross

Dog: One of the four categories or quadrants of the BCG growth-share matrix developed by Boston Consulting Group in the 1970s to manage different business units within a company. A dog is a business unit that has a small market share in a mature industry. It therefore neither generates the strong cash flow nor requires the hefty investment that a cash cow or star unit would (two other categories in the BCG matrix). The term "dog" may also refer to a stock that is a chronic underperformer and hence a drag on the performance of a portfolio.

Daydream: There are two knives, one point-down, one point-up, inside the balloon. The kids were removed and rocks instead were sewn inside the wolf's belly. Collapses of water from the balloons, thrown one after the other, against the barn. The infant is no longer the string of zeroes folded into the water, folded below the water. Water in drops, in strings— in this bag—it simply falls.

White Knight: A white knight is an individual or company that acquires a corporation on the verge of being taken over by forces deemed undesirable by company officials (sometimes referred to as a "black knight"). While the target company doesn't remain independent, a white knight is viewed as a preferred option to the hostile company completing their takeover. Unlike a hostile takeover, current management typically remains in place in a white knight scenario, and investors receive better compensation for their shares.

The white knight is the "savior" of a company in the midst of a hostile takeover. Often a white knight is sought out by company officials—sometimes to preserve the company's core business and other times just to negotiate better takeover terms. An example of the former can be seen in the movie *Pretty Woman* when corporate raider/black knight Edward Lewis (played by Richard Gere) has a change of heart and decides to work with the head of a company he'd originally planned on ransacking.

In addition to white knights and black knights, there is a third potential takeover candidate called a gray knight. As one might guess, a gray knight is not as desirable as a white knight, but more desirable than a black knight.

I didn't know, when I'd never made love, the sounds that I would make then—like that, I didn't know the sound of my fear: cry like the faraway animal. Deep animal moan from somewhere else and a quiet *stay, stay* chanted where the coin's gold edge and the warm night meet. When I was a child I knew the details of each foal's birth—the chestnut, catching her first breath in her mother's shit-covered tail. Her hooves, still soft and curled underneath as a human ear, pawed at the dead udder. When the sun rose on her I thought: could any light be pale lapping onto this world. Could any surface glossed—a bed of snow, the bed of the river—fall flat against the world that holds us in.

▼

Sleeping Beauty: A company that is considered prime for takeover, but has not yet been approached by an acquiring company.

In relation to mergers and acquisitions (M&A), a sleeping beauty is a company that is "sleeping"; that is, one that is ripe for takeover to achieve its full potential. A sleeping beauty might be a new company that has great potential but has not yet been noticed, or it could be an established company that has not been managed well, and is therefore not maximizing its potential. A sleeping beauty essentially lies in wait until a takeover occurs, at which point the company theoretically would be able to live up to its potential.

You laugh sometimes, loving me, you are that happy. And the weather, somewhere. And the milk—it comes in around us. The children we still have are still alive. In the middle, love is temporary.

There is actually very much fragility.

—John of the Cross

Lady Macbeth Strategy: A corporate-takeover strategy in which a third party poses as a white knight to gain trust, but then turns around and joins with unfriendly bidders.

Lady Macbeth, one of Shakespeare's most frightful and ambitious characters, devises a cunning plan for her husband, the Scottish general, to kill Duncan, the King of Scotland. The success of Lady Macbeth's scheme lies in her deceptive ability to appear noble and virtuous, and thereby secure Duncan's trust in the Macbeths' false loyalty.

When the infant is still in me and you are also in me and you pull from me and you are covered in blood, I am the blood and we are all three of us blood—then this is our marriage, held. This is our marriage, flipping and warm in the teeth of the infant.

Furthermore, it would appear that slave prices fluctuate less than do cotton prices. This and the less clear-cut lag of the slave prices make it difficult to accept the image of unwary planters helplessly exposing themselves in a market dominated by speculators. It would make more sense to argue simply that the rising trend of slave prices coupled with a growing slave population is in and of itself strong evidence of the profitability of slavery.

▼

Infants and boats are profitable.

—John of the Cross

Index, deliver me. Index, could you ever hold yourself toward me.

—John of the Cross

▼

Someone delivers the infant while hands wailing follow some other part. Hands of genuine sadness—hands spreading again, granting the body of our four rich handfuls. Earth, this infant is made up of you. Like you, he will die interminably. Earth, I hold myself open toward you. Infant, I am reaching utterly toward you. Earth, someone is holding the infant toward you in the ancient gesture of need.

Daydream: I could say it as simply as this: it was never over. I could say it as simply as this: love is never over. I could say it as simply as this: fragile. Could say: exquisite. Could say: incessant. Could say: the body exploded into bits. I could say it as simply as this: that is what the teeth are for, that is what the bones are for. I could say the years felt fragile. I could say the infants have all felt fragile. I could say the light fell down.

For a male field hand the returns considered will be limited to the sales of products realized from his field labor; in the case of a female hand, an addition must be made for the returns realized on the labor and sale of her children. Because of these basic differences in the production functions for the two sexes, they will be treated separately.

Knowledge Economy: A system of consumption and production that is based on intellectual capital. The knowledge economy commonly makes up a large share of all economic activity in developed countries. In a knowledge economy, a significant part of a company's value may consist of intangible assets, such as the value of its workers' knowledge (intellectual capital). However, generally accepted accounting principles do not allow companies to include these assets on balance sheets.

▼

Index, deliver me from. Deliver me unto.

—John of the Cross

Could I say: the waters washed us clean. Could I say: the world was irradiated and then it turned to glass. Could I say: what counted gave birth to the Index, and we increased.

—John of the Cross

Invisible Hand: A term coined by economist Adam Smith in his 1776 book *An Inquiry into the Nature and Causes of the Wealth of Nations*. In his book he states:

Every individual necessarily labours to render the annual revenue of the society as great as he can. He generally neither intends to promote the public interest, nor knows how much he is promoting it . . . He intends only his own gain, and he is in this, as in many other cases, led by an invisible hand to promote an end which was no part of his intention. Nor is it always the worse for society that it was no part of his intention. By pursuing his own interest he frequently promotes that of the society more effectually than when he really intends to promote it. I have never known much good done by those who affected to trade for the public good.

Daydream: I coin the lavender infant while what is stitched together of our lives, it approaches us. Then worse, the infant is blue while what is attached to our lives, it proliferates. Then worse, the infant is gray while what is severing from our lives, it also proliferates. Then worse, the infant's wire cuts and the more appropriate faith, it spills from us.

Slave-breeding and slave-trading were not generally considered to be high or noble types of activity for a southern gentleman. Indeed, many plantation owners would stoop to all sorts of subterfuge to disguise the fact that they were engaging in any part of the slave trade or breeding operations.

At the marriage bed the places for kissing are also for biting, except for the upper lip, the inside of the mouth, and the eyes. Teeth of good quality are even and of the right size, with shiny reflective surfaces, sharp edges, no chips, and the ability to retain colors. You are coming into us who cannot withstand you. You are coming into us who never wanted to withstand you.

Paris Hilton Stock Index: A stock index comprised of companies associated with the socialite Paris Hilton. Some investors conceive her influence on the consumer spending habits of her fans is material enough to give these companies a competitive advantage.

The concept behind the Paris Hilton Index resides in her endorsements and product lines. Ideally, Hilton's fans see her using certain products or releasing her own brands and flock to purchase the goods. As a result, the companies behind the products experience increased sales. Companies included in this index are Parlux Fragrances (who manufacture Hilton's brand of perfumes) (NASDAQ: PARL), News Corp (NASDAQ: NWS), Time Warner (NYSE: TWC) and Amazon (NASDAQ: AMZN).

Daydream: A string of a billion zeroes in outer space or a string of a billion zeroes in water. The field is a field pulled up out of itself and this field will not help us. This infant had a father and this infant had a mother and this infant had a story and the story had infants and the infants were incessant and the infants were relentless and the infants were unending and the infants were interminable and the infants were insurmountable and the infants were not only the outer space or this still water.

▼

You didn't marry me, my teeth trembling against the doorknob. You didn't feel the same point of the floorboard, or curtains fervent at night—window open—against the low tide. I was moved. Moved to the same latched gate, the same turning, of me, away at the night I curved through. Like no house. It's like no house curves through you.

Under the tinny roof of Songkhla's commercial port, on Thailand's south-east coast, the imperial-blue cargo boat that brought Myint Thein back to shore is unloading its catch, barrel by barrel. The day's international fish trading has just begun, and buyers are milling about in bright yellow rubber boots, running slimy scales between their fingers, as hobbling cats nibble at the fishbones and guts strewn across the pavement.

To make the calculations in this rather complex situation manageable, the following assumptions will be made:

1. Each prime field wench produced five to ten marketable children during her lifetime.
2. The prime field wench was one-half to two-thirds as productive as a prime field hand when she was actually at work in the field.
3. The wench's children began to be productive in field labor at age six, with the males becoming self-sustaining by age nine (that is, they then earned the adult maintenance charge of $20 per year), while females became self-sustaining by age thirteen.
4. The typical wench had as many male as female children.
5. Nursery costs were about $50 per successful pregnancy. The maternity costs have been included in the annual charge for the children's upkeep; similarly, the $16 decline every other year for the first few years in the wench's own field returns represents the allowance for time lost because of pregnancy.

No one was looking for you and then grew forgotten. Put the listening that reached you—no one was also looking at you. What requires you is exactly what you'd like—put the grim one, and then your mother's soul whips.

—John of the Cross

Daydream: The infant's head, softened, pushed down through my torso and out my vagina. Then the neck turning. My brains flowing. My bones softened and split apart. It is the gesture of utterly reaching.

Where the natural increase is shipped off, where the infants are shipped off, where the people are shipped off, where the animals are shipped off, where there is reaching.

—John of the Cross

Wench, my love, my heart, as if goodness didn't hurt to hold. As if opacity didn't hurt to hold. As if pure goodness could not split you, hold you, and then force your deepest part.

But these qualifications do not change the principal conclusion that slavery was apparently about as remunerative as alternative employments to which slave capital might have been put. Large or excessive returns were clearly limited to a few fortunate planters, but apparently none suffered excessively either.

Where there is no excessive suffering. Where there is no excessive suffering. Where there is none, put suffering. Where there is no table, put food, put people. Where there is no table, I am inside the table of excessive suffering. I am in the gesture of utterly reaching. Did the Index do this to the table. Did the Index do this to the suffering. Did none suffer excessively.

—John of the Cross

The membrane we need is inhuman. The earth we need is inhuman. The virus we need is inhuman. The algorithm we need is inhuman. The mind we need is inhuman. The mycelium we need is inhuman. The rhizome we need is inhuman. The animal we need is inhuman. The begging we need is inhuman. The prophet we need is inhuman. The increase we need is inhuman. Index, is this who you are. Is this what you are pointing us toward.

—John of the Cross

On solar system bedsheets, there, behind the sunlight, is the long pressure of an infant's love. Becoming mute with the infant's love. Long influence of stars touched by the hand wrapped, asleep, in the newly laundered sheets. I check: each is alive in his sleep. You are also asleep, at the end of the yarn they are weaving around the edge of a pink paper heart fattening—if quieter, now.

Some spoke frankly about Virginia as a "breeding state," though the reply to such allegations was generally an indignant denial. Whether systematically bred or not, the natural increase of the slave force was an important, probably the most important, product of the more exhausted soil of the Old South. The relationship between the prices of men and women in the slave market, when compared with the ratio of hiring rates for male and female field hands, gives an even stronger indication that the superior usefulness of females of breeding age was economically recognized. The price structure clearly reflects the added value of females due to their ability to generate capital gains.

The Index we need is inhuman. Need: actual radiation. Need: the different kind of mind.

—John of the Cross

Competitive Intelligence: The process of collecting and analyzing information about competitors' strengths and weaknesses in a legal and ethical manner to enhance business decision-making. Competitive intelligence activities can be basically grouped into two main types:

1. Tactical, which is shorter-term and seeks to provide input into issues such as capturing market share or increasing revenues; and
2. Strategic, which focuses on longer-term issues such as key risks and opportunities facing the enterprise.

▼

Put everlastingness. Put unendingness. Put relentlessness. Put algorithms and put operations. Put them everywhere you turn. You will become the field gesturing. You will become fishbones and guts, you will become strewn across the pavement. You will become the bruises along the mind. You will become the weapons-grade membrane. You will become the animals of actual mercy. You will become actual dead animals. You will become dead.

—John of the Cross

"The comfort we need is inhuman" is a line from Bill McKibben

"The horizon is simple: a sheet of light" is a line from Todd Fredson

"This is capitalism at its worst" is from Kevin Bales

"Smear a small red spider / A cleaning fire" is a line from Hoa Nguyen

"Safe through the generous fields" is a line from Lucille Clifton

"You are coming into us who cannot withstand you / you are coming into us who never wanted to withstand you" is a slight variation of Adrienne Rich

Kama Sutra is widely sampled

John of the Cross is widely misquoted

Kate Hodal and Chris Kelly are widely sampled from their *Guardian* article "Trafficked into Slavery on Thai Trawlers to Catch Food for Prawns"

Economic definitions are from the website Investopedia

"Americium" definition is from Wikipedia

Alfred H. Conrad and John R. Meyer's "The Economics of Slavery in the Ante Bellum South" is widely sampled

JOHN ASHBERY
Selected Poems
Self-Portrait in a Convex Mirror

TED BERRIGAN
The Sonnets

LAUREN BERRY
The Lifting Dress

JOE BONOMO
Installations

PHILIP BOOTH
Lifelines: Selected Poems,
*   1950–1999*
Selves

JULIANNE BUCHSBAUM
The Apothecary's Heir

JIM CARROLL
Fear of Dreaming:
*   The Selected Poems*
Living at the Movies
Void of Course

ALISON HAWTHORNE DEMING
Genius Loci
Rope

CARL DENNIS
Another Reason
Callings
New and Selected Poems
*   1974–2004*
Practical Gods
Ranking the Wishes
Unknown Friends

DIANE DI PRIMA
Loba

STUART DISCHELL
Backwards Days
Dig Safe

STEPHEN DOBYNS
Velocities: New and Selected
*   Poems, 1966–1992*

EDWARD DORN
Way More West: New and
*   Selected Poems*

ROGER FANNING
The Middle Ages

ADAM FOULDS
The Broken Word

CARRIE FOUNTAIN
Burn Lake
Instant Winner

AMY GERSTLER
Crown of Weeds:
*   Poems*
Dearest Creature
Ghost Girl
Medicine
Nerve Storm
Scattered at Sea

EUGENE GLORIA
Drivers at the Short-Time
*   Motel*
Hoodlum Birds
My Favorite Warlord

DEBORA GREGER
By Herself
Desert Fathers, Uranium
*   Daughters*
God
Men, Women, and Ghosts
Western Art

TERRANCE HAYES
Hip Logic
How to be Drawn
Lighthead
Wind in a Box

NATHAN HOKS
The Narrow Circle

ROBERT HUNTER
Sentinel and Other Poems

MARY KARR
Viper Rum

WILLIAM KECKLER
Sanskrit of the Body

JACK KEROUAC
Book of Sketches
Book of Blues
Book of Haikus

JOANNA KLINK
Circadian
Excerpts from a Secret
*   Prophecy*
Raptus

JOANNE KYGER
As Ever:
*   Selected Poems*

ANN LAUTERBACH
Hum
If in Time: Selected Poems,
*   1975–2000*
On a Stair
Or to Begin Again
Under the Sign

CORINNE LEE
PYX

PHILLIS LEVIN
May Day
Mercury

PATRICIA LOCKWOOD
Motherland Fatherland
*   Homelandsexuals*

WILLIAM LOGAN
Macbeth in Venice
Madame X
Strange Flesh
The Whispering Gallery

ADRIAN MATEJKA
The Big Smoke
Mixology

MICHAEL MCCLURE
Huge Dreams: San Francisco
*   and Beat Poems*

ROSE MCLARNEY
Its Day Being Gone

DAVID MELTZER
David's Copy: The Selected
*   Poems of David Meltzer*

ROBERT MORGAN
Dark Energy
Terroir

CAROL MUSKE-DUKES
An Octave Above Thunder
Red Trousseau
Twin Cities

ALICE NOTLEY
Culture of One
The Descent of Alette
Disobedience
In the Pines
Mysteries of Small Houses

WILLIE PERDOMO
The Essential Hits of
*   Shorty Bon Bon*

LIA PURPURA
It Shouldn't Have Been
*   Beautiful*

LAWRENCE RAAB
The History of Forgetting
Visible Signs: New and Selected
*   Poems*

BARBARA RAS
The Last Skin
One Hidden Stuff

MICHAEL ROBBINS
Alien vs. Predator
The Second Sex

PATTIANN ROGERS
Generations
Holy Heathen Rhapsody
Wayfare

WILLIAM STOBB
Absentia
Nervous Systems

TRYFON TOLIDES
An Almost Pure Empty Walking

SARAH VAP
Viability

ANNE WALDMAN
Gossamurmur
Kill or Cure
Manatee/Humanity
Structure of the World
*   Compared to a Bubble*

JAMES WELCH
Riding the Earthboy 40

PHILIP WHALEN
Overtime: Selected Poems

ROBERT WRIGLEY
Anatomy of Melancholy and
*   Other Poems*
Beautiful Country
Earthly Meditations: New and
*   Selected Poems*
Lives of the Animals
Reign of Snakes

MARK YAKICH
The Importance of Peeling
*   Potatoes in Ukraine*
Unrelated Individuals Forming
*   a Group Waiting to Cross*

Printed in the United States
by Baker & Taylor Publisher Services